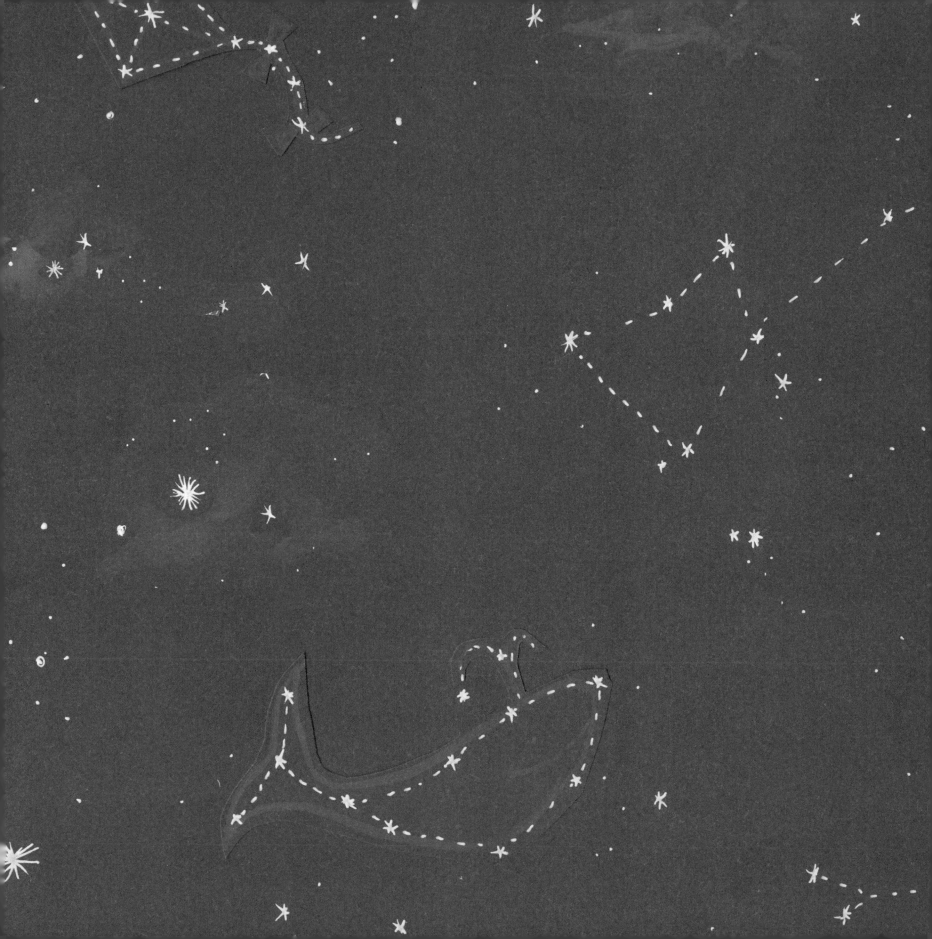

Sweet Dreams

BEDTIME VISUALIZATIONS FOR KIDS

written by
MARIAM GATES

illustrated by
LEIGH STANDLEY

sounds true
BOULDER, COLORADO

For my father, Gordon, who taught me how to tell a great story, and for my son, Dylan, who helped write this one.

—M. G.

For M. G., who taught me about dharma, and for Ruby and Graham, who have become it.

—L. S.

Sounds True
Boulder, CO 80306

Text © 2019 by Mariam Gates
Illustrations © 2019 by Leigh Standley

Published 2019

Book design by Meredith March

Printed in South Korea

Library of Congress Cataloging-in-Publication Data

Names: Gates, Mariam, author. | Standley, Leigh, illustrator.
Title: Sweet dreams : bedtime visualizations for kids /
 by Mariam Gates ; illustrated by Leigh Standley.
Description: Boulder, CO : Sounds True, 2019. | Audience: Age 4-8.
Identifiers: LCCN 2018044448 (print) | LCCN 2018051908 (ebook) |
 ISBN 9781683643319 (ebook) | ISBN 9781683641704 (hardcover)
Subjects: LCSH: Sleep—Juvenile literature. | Children—Sleep—Juvenile
 literature. | Bedtime—Juvenile literature.
Classification: LCC RA786 (ebook) | LCC RA786 .G335 2019 (print) |
 DDC 612.8/210833—dc23
LC record available at https://lccn.loc.gov/2018044448

10 9 8 7 6 5 4 3 2 1

This is a book of ADVENTURES.

Each journey will help you calm your mind and relax your body as you get ready for a peaceful night's rest.

You can fly through space, scuba dive with sea turtles, and shrink down small enough to ride on the back of a butterfly.

Choose where you want to go. You only need to pack your imagination and turn the page.

LET'S BEGIN!

SHRINKING DOWN

Imagine you're in a leafy green rainforest.

Take a DEEP BREATH IN and a
LONG BREATH OUT.

You are going on an adventure, but first
you're going to shrink yourself down to
the size of your pinky.

Start by scrunching your toes and feet.
Take a deep breath in, squeeze them tight,
and then relax as you breathe out. Now
squeeze your feet, legs, stomach, chest,

shoulders, arms, and hands. Make yourself as tight as you can, and then release. One more time: take a big breath in and squeeze everything, even your face, and then let it all go.

You did it! You've made yourself so small! Now you are ready to explore. Reach out to touch a blade of grass. It is as tall as you are now.

You come to a flower stem that is as big as a tree to you. Bend your knees and hold them to your chest. Rock from side to side to shimmy-shimmy up the flower stem.

What does your flower look like?

Climb right in. It is like you're in your own flower house. It smells so sweet inside. Take a DEEP BREATH IN and a LONG BREATH OUT to enjoy the aroma.

A butterfly comes fluttering down to offer you a ride. You climb on and quickly she takes off.

Rock back and forth to glide through the air. Imagine the wind in your hair as you flutter and soar over the rainforest. When you are ready, land gently back on the ground.

To grow big again, take a deep breath in and stretch your whole body—long, long, longer. Breathe out and relax. You are back to your normal size, feeling happy and relaxed.

BLOWING BUBBLES

Lie down on your back and relax. Picture yourself in one of your favorite places.

Where are you? What makes this a wonderful place?

You have a bottle of bubbles and a long wand.

What color is your bubble wand?

Begin to blow big bubbles. Take a deep breath in and blow out bubbles with a WHOOOOOOSH. Take another deep breath in and blow.

So many shiny bubbles go dancing into the air! Reach your hands out to touch them. POP, POP, POP!

Take another deep breath in and blow.

For a moment, you are one of the bubbles. Imagine floating UP, UP, UP. Feel how light you are and how easily you move on the breeze.

When you have gone as high as you want to go, start to sink gently DOWN, DOWN, DOWN until you are settled back on the ground.

You are going to blow bubbles one more time, but this time each bubble carries a wish inside. These happy bubbles travel far and wide.

Who do you want to send
a wish bubble to?

Get ready, TAKE A BREATH IN,
and BLOW!

Rocketing to the Moon

Lie down on your back and bring your legs together, pressing your arms tight against your body. You are a rocket ship going to the moon.

Start bouncing your legs to ignite the engine.
10 . . . 9 . . . 8 . . . 7 . . . 6 . . .

Now shake, shake, shake your whole body.
5 . . . 4 . . . 3 . . . 2 . . . 1. BLAST OFF!!!

As you launch into space, point your toes and make yourself as long as you can.

Take a DEEP BREATH IN and a LONG
BREATH OUT. Relax your whole body as
you sail through space. You are heading
toward the moon.

All around you are bright stars and clusters
of asteroids. It's peaceful and quiet.

The moon is getting bigger and bigger the
closer you get.

Thud. YOU HAVE ARRIVED.

Step out of your rocket. Bend and extend
your legs to make big steps onto the moon
like you are walking in slow motion.

You can see Earth in the distance. It is blue and green, like a jewel hanging in the dark sky. Take some deep breaths in and out and think about Earth and how beautiful it is. Think about how lucky you are to live on such a wonderful planet.

It's time to climb back into your rocket ship.

Take another DEEP BREATH IN and a LONG BREATH OUT.

YOU ARE HEADING HOME.

MAKING IT RAIN

You are going to make it rain.

Lie down on your back and imagine you can hear a light rain just starting outside. Rub your hands together, palm to palm, to make the sound.

Then comes the pitter-patter of raindrops. Snap or tap your fingertips together to make the pitter-patter sound.

Now the storm is picking up and the rain is getting louder. Start clapping your hands for the bigger raindrops.

The rain is coming down harder. Thwack your hands on your thighs as the heavier rain comes.

THERE'S THUNDER NOW!

Pound your hands on the bed or floor.

But soon the storm is starting to shift. Bring your hands back to your thighs—thwack, thwack, thwack. And the rain is changing. Go back to your clapping. The storm is letting up. Start tapping or snapping your fingers again. It has almost moved past. Rub your hands together for the lightest raindrops.

Now stop making any sound at all.

Take a DEEP BREATH IN and a LONG BREATH OUT.

Listen to the silence. Feel how quiet and still the world is now that the storm has passed.

GALLOPING THROUGH A MEADOW

Imagine you are in a meadow. The sun is shining and the air is warm on your skin.

You hear a light rustling and feel a soft, wet nose nuzzling your neck. A friendly horse is trying to say hello.

What is the horse's name?

The horse bends down low so you can easily climb on. Reach your hands way out to each side to get on her back.

Hold onto her mane. Kick your heels gently to tell her you are ready to go.

Squeeze your knees to your chest. Then kick your legs in the air as the horse starts to gallop through the fields. There's a line of bushes ahead. You're going to jump them! Kick, kick, kick until she leaps. Now grab your knees tight to your chest again and then release. YOU MADE IT!

When you are done with your ride, slow your horse gently by walking your feet up and down, and then stop. Slide down her back onto the earth.

Give your horse a warm hug of thanks.
Wrap your arms across your body and squeeze tight.

DIVING
UNDERWATER

Imagine you are a scuba diver in an underwater world.

Wearing your scuba gear, you can breathe underwater! Take a DEEP BREATH IN and a LONG, RELAXING BREATH OUT.

Notice how light you feel in the water. With just a flick of your flippers you can swim in any direction you like. Try kicking your flippers one at a time.

Seaweed sways around you. Move your body back and forth—loose and wavy like seaweed.

Shiny fish peep in and out of the rocks around you. Blue, yellow, orange, and purple fish swim by. A clownfish darts out and then back into his home.

Above you, a large speckled turtle moves slowly by. Press the soles of your feet together with your knees out to the sides. Move your arms and knees in and out to swim like the turtle.

You decide to swim up to the surface. Now you are floating easily on the top of the water. A pod of dolphins dives and plays nearby.

Take a DEEP BREATH IN and a LONG BREATH OUT. What an ADVENTURE!

FLYING A KITE

Imagine the wide, blue sky above you. You are in a park surrounded by rolling hills.

Who is there with you on this fun day?

Reach your hands out in front of you to grab . . .
A KITE!

What does your kite look like?

Hold onto your kite string with both hands and lift your legs into the air to start running.

Keep running and feel the tug of the kite lifting UP, UP, UP in the sky. Now place your feet back down on the ground.

Sway your arms back and forth as your kite dances in the wind high above.

Now imagine you are the kite. Extend your arms and legs out to the sides as wide as you can. Feel what it is like to be that beautiful kite gliding through the air.

Take a DEEP BREATH IN and a LONG BREATH OUT.

The sky is full of colorful kites, swirling and flying in the sunshine.

When you are ready, bring your kite all the way back to the ground. Feel your body settle and relax.

SWEET DREAMS

Now it is time to settle in for the night.

Get into bed. As you lie on your back, notice every point where your body is resting on the bed. Feel how soft and comfortable it is.

Bring your attention to your feet. Then notice the backs of your legs, your waist, and your back. How do your shoulders feel? Let your attention travel all the way down your arms. Let your hands be quiet and still. Feel the back of your head resting on your pillow.

Take a DEEP BREATH IN and a LONG BREATH OUT.
Breathe in and out again.

See if you can relax your whole body a little more. Imagine you are a melting ice cream cone on a warm day.

Breathe in and fill with air . . . Breathe out and relax . . .
Breathe in peace and breathe out anything that worries you.
Breathe in softness and breathe out anything that
feels hard or tight in your body.

Breathe in and fill yourself with air.
Breathe out and let go.

SWEET DREAMS.